Seals

Baby Animals™

ALICE TWINE

PowerKiDS press™

New York

For Nora and Annie Quesnell and Hailey Power

Published in 2008 by The Rosen Publishing Group, Inc.
29 East 21st Street, New York, NY 10010

First Edition

Editor: Amelie von Zumbusch
Book Design: Julio Gil
Photo Researcher: Nicole Pristash

Photo Credits: Cover, p. 1 © Norbert Rosing/Getty Images; p. 5 © SuperStock, Inc.; pp. 7, 9, 11, 13, 15, 17, 19, 21, 23, 24 (top left, top right, bottom left, bottom right) © www.shutterstock.com.

Library of Congress Cataloging-in-Publication Data

Twine, Alice.
  Seals / Alice Twine. — 1st ed.
      p. cm. — (Baby·animals)
  Includes index.
  ISBN-13: 978-1-4042-3773-5 (lib. bdg.) ISBN-10: 1-4042-3773-9 (lib. bdg.)
  1. Seals (Animals)—Infancy—Juvenile literature. I. Title.
  QL737.P64T85 2008
  599.79—dc22
                                            2006038379

Manufactured in the United States of America.

Contents

Baby seals are called pups.
Mother seals take good care
of their pups. Seal pups drink
their mother's milk.

Seals are good swimmers. They use their back **flippers** to push themselves through the water.

Some seal pups can swim when they are first born. Other seal pups learn to swim when they are several weeks old.

Seal pups can dive down hundreds of feet (m) under water. However, they have to come up to the **surface** to breathe.

Most seal pups are born on beaches. Some pups live on a beach with a seal **colony** for several months after they are born.

13

There are many kinds of seals.
This pup is a harbor seal.
Harbor seals are also called
common seals.

15

Baby harp seals, like this pup, have white fur. As a harp seal grows up, its **coat** will turn darker.

This pup is an elephant seal. Elephant seals are the biggest kind of seal. They can grow up to 15 feet (5 m) long.

Baby sea lions are also called pups. Sea lions are related to seals. Unlike seals, sea lions can walk on their front flippers.

Young eared seals are also called pups. Eared seals have "seal" in their name, but they are not true seals. They are more like sea lions.

Words to Know

coat

colony

flipper

surface

Index

Web Sites

Due to the changing nature of Internet links, PowerKids Press has developed an online list of Web sites related to the subject of this book. This site is updated regularly. Please use this link to access the list: www.powerkidslinks.com/baby/seals/

24